"How To Be a Thief!"

"7 Easy Ways To Break In Any Where!"

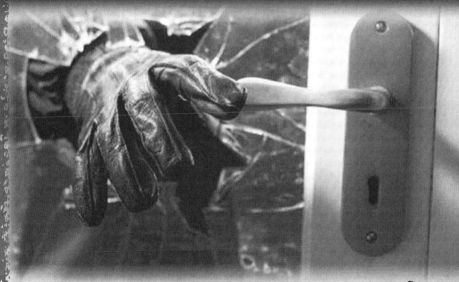

Learn-How-To Pick Locks Overnight Guaranteed or Your Money Back!

First things first. This is for informational purposes only. The only house you (should) be picking is your house ;-). If you do get caught picking a house trouble will find you Unless you can run very fast. I personally don't recommend you DO THAT sort of thing because its against the law. If you were going to pick a lock (yours of-course) theres three very simple and effective methods you can use depending on the security you currently have.

HERE'S a BONUS: I also included some bonus material like **how to Mac Giver yourself out of police cuffs**, **how to drill any lock open**, or even **how to break in locks using only a pepsi can**. Just my way of saying thank you for buying this book.

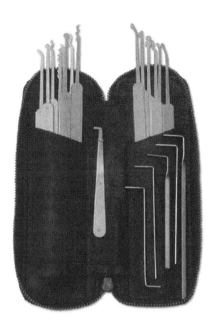

First method I am going to go into is Picking. The first time I tried picking I did it on a deadbolt and I got the deadbolt open in seconds. The second time it took about 20 minutes lol. After doing it for about a week I could easily get any deadbolt on my house open in about 7 - 12 seconds. All it takes is practice and knowing the fundamentals to picking.

I personally recommend buying your self a pair of picks rather then trying to use bobby pens like in the movies. Get the right tool for the job and it will go much smoother.

when you buy your set you'll get a basic set of two items, torque wrenches and pickers.

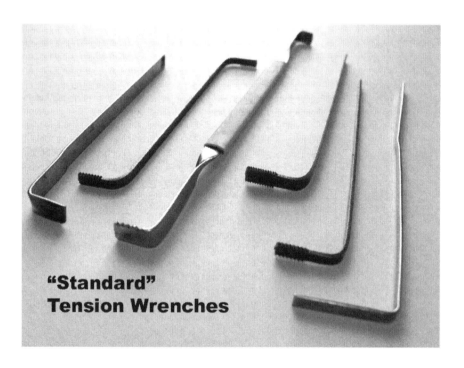

"Standard"
Tension Wrenches

Here's a Tension wrench, its main purpose is to keep enough pressure on the pins to hold them in place after you scrap across them. without the tension wrench you will NOT be able to pick.

How To Use Tension wrench:

1. Below is a torque wrench inserted into a door lock. You will insert teh torque wrench in at a 90 degree angle.

2. You will slowly press the torque wrench down or pull up. You should feel the lock give or not give. You want to turn the wrench in the direction that teh lock gives to.

3. Now you will keep that pressure and continue to press that pressure without ever giving back. If you do give

back you will have to start all over when you start to

pick

Setting a pin is the act of lifting a pin stack to the

shear line (correct height) in a way that causes it to stay

there. Once a pin is set, we can move on the next. When we set all of the pins in the lock, it will open. The way to make the pins stay set after correct lifting is to apply **tension**. Tension is the lock-picking term for putting rotational pressure on the plug.

After the wrench has taken all the pressure it can take you will enter your pick and start to stick the pick all the way down the key hole and sweep back 3 times while keeping the pressure down.

The reason why I sweep back 3 times is sometimes you'll get lucky and get 3 or 5 of the pins by sweeping back and forth.

The trick is to understand that you can only set the pin that is binding at that time. You can't just choose any pin and lift it under tension to make it *click*. Once you set a pin, another will bind. Continue this same process until the lock is completely picked. The sequence in which the pins bind (and hence must be set) is called the **binding order** and is unique to each lock.

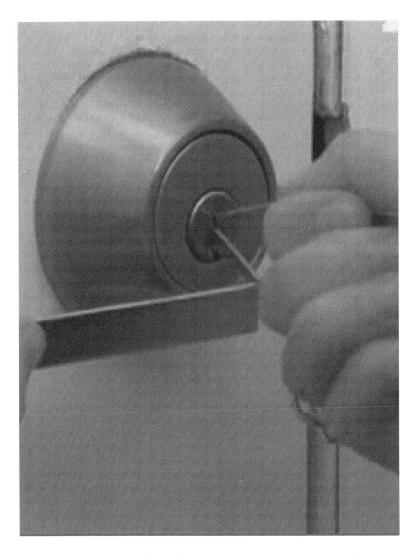

the act of individually lifting pins up in order to "set"

them. Getting comfortable holding the pick is the first

step in being able to feel your way around the inside of a

lock. The most common "proper" way to do this is like a

pencil with your index (or middle in my case) finger

resting on the top of the pick's shaft

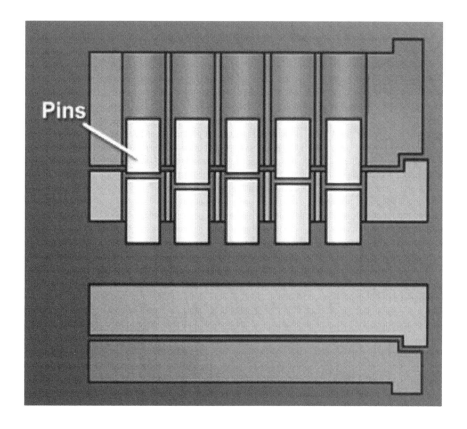

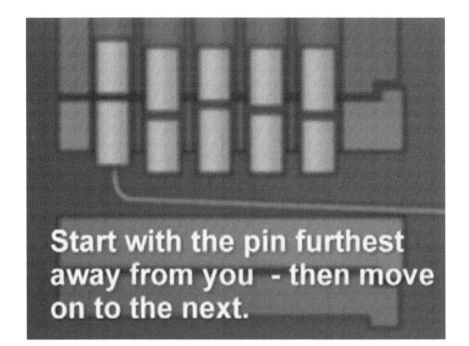

Start with the pin furthest away from you - then move on to the next.

Before you start, "rake" the lock a few times.

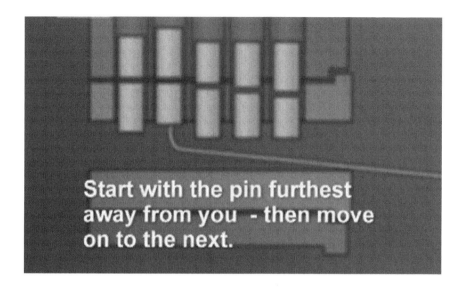

Start with the pin furthest away from you - then move on to the next.

Inside View of Picking.

I actually try to visualize the pins I am doing when picking a lock. Kind of like trying to find the light switch when its pitch dark. As soon as you get a baring in the room you can easily get an idea of where the light should be. Some people are better at picking then others because they are what you call

KINESTHETIC. Kinesthetic learning (also known as

tactile learning) is a learning style in which learning

takes place by the student carrying out a physical activity,

rather than listening to a lecture or watching a

demonstration. People with a preference for kinesthetic

learning are also commonly known as "do-ers". Tactile-

kinesthetic learners make up about five percent of the

population.

If your not kinesthetic.. Don't worry it just takes practice.

10 hours of practice and you should be a pro.

Starting from the back of the lock and pulling outward while keeping a loose grip on the pick will allow its tip to ride over the pin tips. Try counting them without lifting anything; then try moving from pin to pin while keeping track of which one you're on. By practicing this sort of thing enough, you'll eventually be able to just choose a pin and know exactly how far into the lock it is.

Opening a Door With a Credit Card

Opening Doors with a credit card can be easy. You Need to things a Jam cannot be in the way and it can not have a dead bolt. If you have a Jam or dead bolt use bump key or a pick.

Here is a dead bolt and credit card, it WONT work.

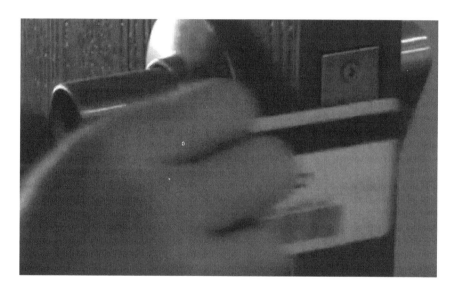

Heres a credit card and regular lock that 99% of house holds have (this will work)!

If the sloped side of the latch isn't facing you, you'll need a hooked tool or long piece of plastic.

Easy pickings... no Door Jam just slide the credit card in and pull the door open. (this is actually the first way I learned to break in doors. (of course its was my own doors as I would never do anything illegal) I used a card I didn't care about so I naturally used a Block

Busters Video Card.

PICKING With A CARD

Defiantly want to make sure the card is laminated of

some type. Soft cards will break and might only be good

for one use. If you get yourself a good laminated card it

can be used over and over again. The card shouldn't be to

hard as it wont be flexible enough to bend around the

hard to get locks.

Credit card with door jam. Still possible to break in just must have the right card. The card must be flexible to bend around two 90 degree corners. If your using a credit card it will break. I recommend Block buster Cards. There free and flexible.

One of my favorite ways to break in is The Bump Key

Its one of my favorites because I can literally teach a child to do it in 5 seconds or less on how to get into 95% of all houses and dead bolts. All you do with a bump key is insert one of 4 bump keys into a lock and literally Bump it or "hit it" and it will jar all the pins up and then you time the pins jumping and turn the key. Wala your in.

You can make your own bump key, I do recommend buying a mechanically tuned one though as there will be no human error in the filing. A bump key basically has every pit of the key filed down to the lowest point. You can see in the pic below.

I don't recommend filing your bump key down yourself. Sure you can do it.

the probability of your filed down key working is probably about 70% of the time. The mechanically tuned key that you can buy will work 100% of the time because there is now human error.

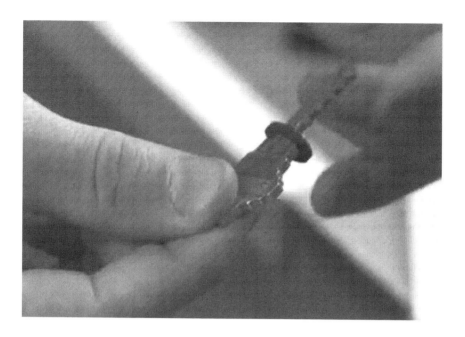

Your secret tool for bumping is a 1/16 rubber washer.
This aligns the key for you automatically after ever time
you bump it.

You can see the photo shows a hammer to bump the key.
I recommend using a hair brush or 1 by 2 piece of wood.

When you bump the pins up all you have to do is
time the turn of the key and Wala door opens.. only takes
like 5 minutes to get a hand of this. The biggest thing is

you'll need a bump key for every big brand thats being

sold. Right now there are only two big brands being sold

by Walmart and Lowes.

Tools You'll Need:

Picking set which you can get: Which will pick any lock
Go ahead and Click here

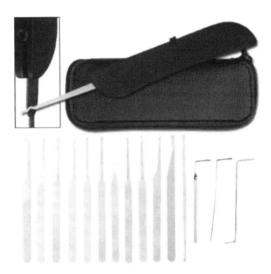

Bump Keys: All the Bump Keys you'll Ever need. [Go ahead and Click here](#)

How To Pick Hand Cuffs

I'm gonna show you how to escape from a set of

professional handcuffs just like the famous escape artist

huodini needed this is for entertainment only and

should never be used to escape from the police any trained law enforcement officer.

Here's a set of smith and wesson model one hundred double locking in cuffs now all you need is a regular bobby pins.

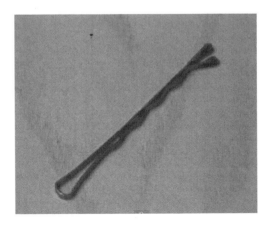

you want to peel away the plastic protective covering on the

into the body can sort of work right now after you've removed

the concealed body pain you want to open it up at the end of

the bobby pin in the keyhole and bend it one way

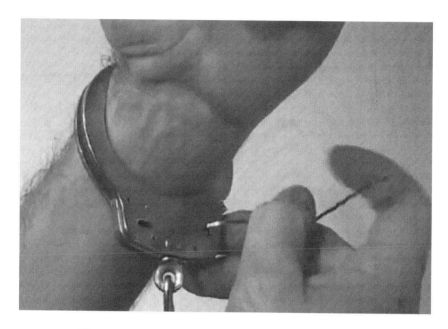

Then take it out and then did the other way tighten

end up with an angle

shape it looks just like

this.

Let me show

you a close-up of how

the body can actually

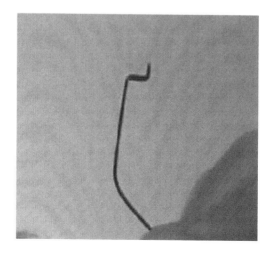

unlocks the handcuffs insert the body pain in the keyhole

and i'm a very edgy you want to take the bobby-pin and bend

it down this will release the ratchet which will alternate cuffs

self a pin double locked you just put the bobby pin in the

keyhole on the other side release the double lock and then

turn it around to release

the ratchet an open the

draw as you can see

here

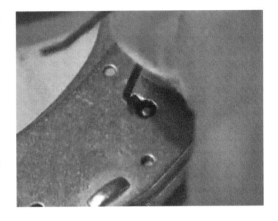

I'm handcuffed in

tight and about five

seconds i've opened up the handcuffs and that's one simple

way that escape artists unlock handcuffs

"How To Break Into a Lock"

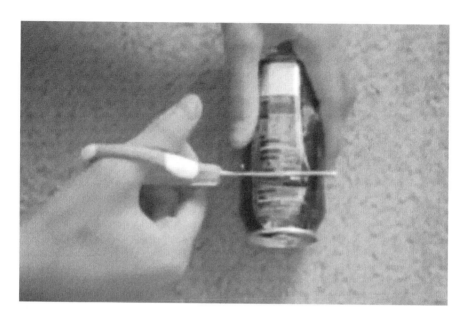

Get A Pepsi Can and cut a rectangular like this.

Now with that rectangle cut a "M" shape into it. This will allow us to shim the lock.

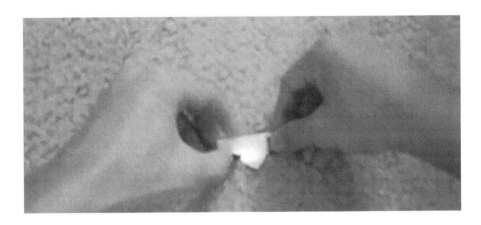

How fold up the lower tabs to allow the shim or

triangle to "point" out.

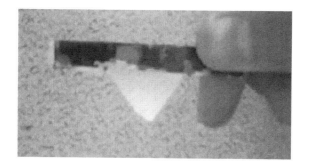

Now fold the top tin down over the taps you just

moved to give you a solid handle like this.

Wrap your shim around the lock with the point on

the inside. Push down the shim as far as you can

and now while pushing down the shim pull up the

lock and Wala.

Tools You'll Need:

Picking set which you can get: Which will pick any lock
Go ahead and Click here

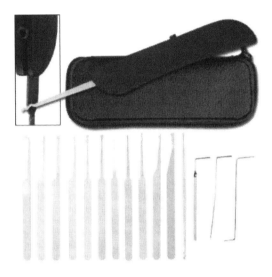

Bump Keys: All the Bump Keys you'll Ever need. Go ahead and Click here

Made in the USA
Las Vegas, NV
08 December 2022

61566760R00020